A Little Book

– of –

Welsh
Quotations

Compiled By
Meic Stephens

Appletree Press

First published in 1997 by
The Appletree Press Ltd, 19-21 Alfred Street,
Belfast, BT2 8DL

Tel: ++44 (0) 1232 243074
Fax: ++44 (0) 1232 246756

A Little Book of Welsh Quotations

A catalogue record for this book
is available from The British Library.

ISBN 0-86281-684-x

9 8 7 6 5 4 3 2 1

Introduction

*W*ales has two languages and two literatures. Literature in Welsh dates from the sixth century and has a rich tradition which survives today as the art at which the Welsh still excel. Welsh literature in English is more recent and was the choice of writers such as Henry Vaughan and Dylan Thomas.

A Little Book of Welsh Quotations selects from both of these literary traditions, drawing on what has been said about Wales and its people by the Welsh themselves and also quoting Roman, Norman, English and American opinions. Most of the authors quoted have been friendly towards Wales, though some, baffled or exasperated by its people's ways, have not been so complimentary. It makes little difference to the Welsh, they know they are a people quite unlike their English neighbours and are always ready to celebrate their Welshness. This little book is an entertaining, informative and stimulating anthology of the country which the visitor to Wales will enjoy for its scope and charm. The quotations reflect the tumultuous history of Wales and can be enjoyed by reading from start to finish, or dipped into for the sheer pleasure of making the acquaintance of new writers and sharing their delight in *Cymru*, the land of the Welsh.

*A*ll the Britons paint themselves with woad, which gives their skin a bluish colour and makes them look very dreadful in battle.

Julius Caesar c.102-44 BC

De Bello Gallico

*T*he Silures were not easily quelled. Neither lenity nor rigorous measures could induce them to submit.

Tacitus c.55-c.120

Annales

*T*he druids were ranged in order, with hands uplifted, invoking the gods and pouring forth horrible imprecations. The strangeness of the sight struck the Romans with awe and terror.

Tacitus c.55-120

Annales

*F*or the kinsman of yonder strangue-tongued man whose voice I heard across the river setting on his dogs will obtain possession of this place, and it will be theirs, and they will hold it in ownership.

Beuno 5th-6th cent

Llyfr Ancr Llanddewibrefi

*I*t is to this day the fashion among the Britons to reckon the faith and religion of Englishmen as naught and to hold no more converse with them than with the heathen.

Bede c.673-735

Historia Ecclesiastica Gentis Anglorum

*F*ee, fie, fo, fum,
I smell the blood of a British man!

Anonymous 9th century

*T*his nation, O King, may now, as in former times, be harassed, and in a great measure weakened and destroyed by your and other powers, and it will also prevail by its laudable exertions, but it can never be totally subdued through the wrath of man, unless the wrath of God shall concur. Nor do I think that any other nation than this of Wales, or any other language, whatever may hereafter come to pass, shall on the day of severe judgement before the Supreme Judge, answer for this corner of the earth.

An Old Man of Pencader 1163

Giraldus Cambrensis, Descriptio Kambriae

A people called Welsh, so bold and
ferocious that, when unarmed, they do not
fear to encounter an armed force, being
ready to shed their blood in defence of
their country, and to sacrifice their lives
for renown.

Henry II c.1165
letter to the Emperor of Byzantium

*M*y fellow countrymen, the Welsh,
although wholly treacherous to everyone --
to each other as well as to foreigners --
covet freedom, neglect peace, are warlike
and skilful in arms, and are eager
for revenge.

Walter Map c.1140-c.1209
De Nugis Curialum

They are as easy to overcome in a single battle as they are difficult to subdue in a protracted war.

Giraldus Cambrensis c.1146-1223

Descriptio Kambriae

If they would be inseparable, they would be insuperable.

Giraldus Cambrensis c.1146-1223

Descriptio Kambriae

The English fight for power, the Welsh for liberty; the one to procure gain, the other to avoid loss; the English hirelings for money, the Welsh patriots for their country.

Giraldus Cambrensis c.1146-1223

Descriptio Kambriae

*T*hey do not engage in marriage until they have tried, by previous cohabitation, the disposition, and particularly the fecundity, of the person with whom they are engaged.

Giraldus Cambrensis c. 1146-1223

Descriptio Kambriae

*N*o one of this nation ever begs, for the houses of all are common to all, and they consider liberality and hospitality among the first virtues.

Giraldus Cambrensis c.1146-1223

Descriptio Kambriae

*T*he King's host came without warning upon Llywelyn ap Gruffudd and slew him and many of his host on the feast day of Pope Damaseus, the eleventh day of the month of December, a Friday, and then all Wales was cast to the ground.

Anonymous 1282

Brenhinedd y Saesson

*W*hen elsewhere it is summer, it is winter in Wales.

Pierre de Langtoft fl. 14th century

Histoire d'Angleterre

*V*ery many said that Owain Glyndwr died; the seers say that he did not.

Anonymous 1416

Annals of Owain Glyndwr

*B*eware of Wales, Christ Jesus
must us keep,
That it make not our child's child to weep.

Anonymous c.1436

The Libel of English Policy

*T*he people of the dominion of Wales have
and do daily use a speech nothing like nor
consonant to the natural mother tongue
used within this realm. . . .No person or
persons that use the Welsh speech or
language shall have or enjoy any manor,
office or fees within the realm of England,
Wales or other the king's dominions upon
pain of forfeiting the same offices or fees
unless he or they use and exercise the
speech or language of English.

Anonymous 1536

Act of Union

*I*f you do not wish to be worse than animals, obtain learning in your own language; if you do not wish to be more unnatural than any other nation under the sun, love your language and those who love it.

William Salesbury c.1520-1584?

Oll Synnwyr Pen Kembero Ygyd

*Y*ou will have some people, as soon as they see the Severn or the belfries of Shrewsbury, and hear an Englishman say goodmorrow, who begin to abandon their Welsh.

Gruffydd Robert pre-1532-post-1598

Dosparth byrr ar y rhan gyntaf o ramadeg Gymraeg

O Cambria, stretch and strain thy
utmost breath
To praise and pray for Queen Elizabeth.

Morris Kyffin c.1555-1598

The Blessedness of Britain

*B*ut I will never be a truant, love,
Till I have learned thy language, for thy
  tongue
Makes Welsh as sweet as ditties highly
  penn'd
Sung by a fair queen in a summer's bower,
With ravishing division, to her lute.

William Shakespeare 1564-1616

Henry IV, part I

*T*hough the nation be said to be
unconquered and most loving liberty, yet it
was never mutinous, and please your
majesty, but stout, valiant, courteous,
hospitable, temperate, ingenious, capable
of all good arts, most lovingly constant,
charitable, great antiquaries, religious
preservers of their gentry and genealogy, as
they are zealous and knowing in religion.

Ben Jonson 1572-1637
For the Honour of Wales

*T*heir Lord they shall praise,
Their language they shall keep,
Their land they shall lose,
Except wild Wales.

Anonymous 1621

*W*ales is fading, the bards are in
their graves.

Anonymous 1627

*T*here were three jovial Welshmen,
    As I have heard men say,
And they would go a'hunting, boys,
    Upon St David's Day;
And all the day they hunted,
    But nothing could they find
Except a ship a'sailing,
    A'sailing with the wind.

Anonymous c.1632

*A*n old and haughty nation proud in arms.

John Milton 1608-74
Comus

I do observe, it being St David's Day, the
picture of a man, dressed like a Welshman,
hanging by the neck upon one of the poles,
which is one of the oddest sights I have
seen in a good while.

Samuel Pepys 1633-1703
Diary

*T*he guile and softness of the Saxon race
In gallant Briton's soul had never place;
Strong as his rocks and in his language
  pure,
In his own innocence and truth secure:
Such is the bold, the noble mountaineer,
As void of treason as he is of fear.

The Brogyntin Poet c.1690

On the Welsh

A Welsh woman? Prithee, of what country's
  that?
– That, Sir, is a country in the world's
backside
Where every man is born a gentleman and
  a genealogist.

John Vanbrugh 1664-1726

Aesop

*T*he devil lives in the middle of Wales.

Daniel Defoe 1660-1731
*A Tour through the Whole Island of Great
Britain*

I have seen no part of England so pleasant for sixty or seventy miles together as those parts of Wales I have been in; and most of the inhabitants are indeed ripe for the Gospel. I mean (if the expression appears strange) they are earnestly desirous of being instructed in it, and as utterly ignorant of it are as any Creek or Cherokee Indians.

John Wesley 1703-91
Diary

*F*or I am of the seed of the Welch woman and speak the truth from my heart.

Christopher Smart 1722-71
Jubilate Agno

*T*he false historians of a polished age
Show that the Saxon has not lost his rage;
Though tamed by arts, his rancour still
   remains:
Beware of Saxons still, ye Cambrian swains.

        Evan Evans (Ieuan Fardd) 1731-88
             The Love of our Country

*A*t Pembroke in the evening we had the
most elegant congregation I have seen
since we came into Wales. Some of them
came in dancing and laughing as into a
theatre, but their mood was quickly
changed and in a few minutes they were as
serious as my subject–Death.

            John Wesley 1703-91
                Journal

*T*his combination of mountainous scenery
is truly sublime and surpasses any thing
I have seen.

J M W Turner 1775-1851
Diary of a Tour in Part of Wales

*P*istyll Rhaeadr and Wrexham steeple,
Snowdon's mountain without its people,
Overton's yew-trees, St Winifred's wells,
Llangollen's bridge and Gresford's bells.

Anonymous late 18th century
The Seven Wonders of North Wales

How oft, in spirit, have I turned to thee,
O sylvan Wye! thou wanderer through
   the woods,
How often has my spirit turned to thee!

William Wordsworth 1770-1850

Lines composed a few miles above

Tintern Abbey

The inhabitants of western Monmouthshire
unwillingly hold intercourse with the
English, retain their ancient prejudices and
still brand them with the name of Saxons.

William Coxe 1747-1828

An Historical Tour through Monmouthshire

*T*he sudden decline of the national minstrelsy and customs of Wales is in a great degree to be attributed to the fanatick imposters, or illiterate plebian preachers, who have too often been suffered to over-run the country, misleading the greater part of the common people from their lawful church, and dissuading them from their innocent amusements, such as singing, dancing, and other rural sports, with which they had been accustomed to delight in from the earliest times. The consequence is, Wales, which was formerly one of the merriest and happiest countries in the world, is now become one of the dullest.

Edward Jones 1752-1824

The Bardic Museum

On the whole, the pleasure of a tour in Wales is in some degree tinged with melancholy, on observing the honest and amiable manners of its inhabitants, to find so many appearances of a fallen country.

Benjamin Heath Malkin 1769-1842
The Scenery, Antiquities, and Biography of
South Wales

Wales yields not, in the shadow of a thought, to England, in loyalty to the reigning family. Indeed, the King seems to be the only Saxon to whom they are thoroughly reconciled.

Benjamin Heath Malkin 1769-1842
The Scenery, Antiquities, and Biography of
South Wales

*S*teal, if possible, my revered friend, one summer from the cold hurry of business, and come to Wales.

Percy Bysshe Shelley 1792-1822

letter to William Godwin

*S*amaria? What was Samaria? Samaria was their ash-tip. An ash-tip where they threw all their sticks and rubbish. A hotbed of Paganism and heresy and everything. Yes, my friends, Samaria was the Merthyr Tydfil of the Land of Canaan.

David Rowland 1795-1862

sermon c. 1835

*I*t is remarkable how fluently little boys and girls can speak Welsh.

Alfred, Lord Tennyson 1850-96

letter to Emily Sellwood

I know not on the face of the earth a region more beautiful, more blissful, and all in all more desirable than the land of Wales.

Thomas Price (Carnhuanawc) 1787-1848
Hanes Cymru

I have walked thrice up Snowdon, which I found very much easier to accomplish than walking on level ground.

Alfred, Lord Tennyson 1850-96
letter to Edmund Lushington

*T*he Welsh language is a vast drawback to Wales, and a manifold barrier to the moral progress and commercial prosperity of the people. It is not easy to over estimate its evil effects.

Anonymous 1847
Report on the State of Education in Wales

*W*ho list to read the deeds
   by valiant Welshmen done
Shall find them worthy men of arms
   as breathes beneath the sun;
they are of valiant hearts,
   of nature kind and meek,
an honour on St David's Day
   it is to wear the Leek.

Anonymous 1851

The Praise of St David's Day

*T*he calm sea shines, loose hang the
   vessel's sails;
Before us are the sweet green fields of
   Wales,
And overhead the cloudless sky of May.

Matthew Arnold 1822-88

Tristram and Iseult

*T*he name of John Jones is in Wales a
perpetual incognito.

Anonymous 1853

Report of the Registrar General

*E*dward the king, the English king,
　　Rode on a milk-white charger;
'I wish to know the worth,' said he,
　　'Of my Welsh lands over the border.
Is the grass rich for sheep and ox,
　　Are the soil and rivers good,
And are my provinces watered well
　　By rebel patriots' blood?'

János Arany 1817-82

A Welski Bard

*T*he old land of my fathers is dear to me,
  Land of poets and singers, men of
  renown;
Her brave warriors, patriots most excellent,
  Spilt their blood for freedom.

Evan James 1809-78

Hen Wlad fy Nhadau

*S*till do the great mountains remain,
  And the winds above them roar.
To the customs of old Wales
  Changes come from year to year;
Every generation fails,
  One has gone, the next is here.
After a lifetime tempest-tossed
  Alun Mabon is no more.
But the language is not lost
  And the old songs yet endure.

John Ceiriog Hughes 1832-87

Alun Mabon

*A*ll conquered people are suspicious of their conquerors. The English have forgot that they ever conquered the Welsh, but some ages will elapse before the Welsh forget that the English have conquered them.

George Borrow 1803-81
Wild Wales

*W*herever I have been in Wales, I have experienced nothing but kindness and hospitality, and when I return to my own country I will say so.

George Borrow 1803-81
Wild Wales

*T*he Welsh language is the curse of Wales.

Anonymous
editorial in *The Times* 1866

On this side Wales -- Wales, where the past still lives. Where every place has its tradition, every name its poetry, and where the people, the genuine people, still knows this past, this tradition, this poetry, and lives with it, and clings to it; while, alas, the prosperous Saxon on the other side, the invader from Liverpool and Birkenhead, has long forgotten his.

Matthew Arnold 1822-88

On the Study of Celtic Literature

It must always be the desire of a government to render its dominions, as far as possible, homogeneous. Sooner or later the difference of language between Wales and England will probably be effaced, an event which is socially and politically so desirable.

Matthew Arnold 1822-88
On the Study of Celtic Literature

Wales, sweet Wales. I believe I must have Welsh blood. I always feel so happy and natural and at home among the kindly Welsh.

Francis Kilvert 1840-79
Diary

*L*ovely the woods, waters, meadows,
 combes, vales,
All the air things wear that build this world
 of Wales;
Only the inmate does not correspond.

Gerard Manley Hopkins 1844-89

In the Valley of the Elwy

I affirm that Welsh nationality is as great a
reality as English nationality.

William Ewart Gladstone 1809-98

speech at Swansea

*A*ll Wales is a sea of song.

John Ceiriog Hughes 1832-87

Yr Oriau Olaf

In North Wales we measure a man from his chin up.

David Lloyd George 1863-45

speech

The Welsh people are an animated, gesticulating people.

Walt Whitman 1819-92

letter to Ernest Rhys

The Nonconformists of Wales are the people of Wales.

William Ewart Gladstone 1809-98

speech

If someone says that we are a nation equal and not subjected to the English, then why have we no Welsh Parliament?

Robert Ambrose Jones (Emrys ap Iwan)

1848-1906

*T*he flag of morn in conqueror's state
   Enters at the English gate;
The vanquished eve, as night prevails,
   Bleeds upon the road to Wales.

A E Housman 1859-1936

The Welsh Marches

*T*he Wales of the future must be a
free Wales

Ben Bowen 1878-1903

Williams Pantycelyn

I would sooner go to Hell than to Wales.

H H Asquith 1852-1928

Speech

It's worth turning exile now and then
   And from little Wales to go,
In order to come back to Wales
   And be able to love her more.

Eliseus Williams (Eifion Wyn) 1867-1926

Y Llanw

Socialism means that the land of Wales will again belong to its people.

Keir Hardie 1856-1915

Socialism and the Celt

And yet I sing my country,
    for Wales shall one day be
the happiest and loveliest land,
    a time when we shall see
no violent hand to waste her,
    no coward to betray her,
no quarrelling to weaken her,
    and when Wales shall be free.

John Morris-Jones 1864-1929

Cymru Fydd

Can I forget the sweet days that have been,
    When poetry first began to warm my
    blood;
When from the hills of gwent I saw
the earth
    Burned into two by Severn's flood?

W H Davies 1871-1940

Days that have been

Stick it, the Welsh!

Anonymous
battle-cry, First World War

Make me content
With some sweetness
From Wales
Whose nightingales
Have no wings.

Edward Thomas 1878-1917
Words

The Welshman has many vices and
drinking is not one of them.

Caradoc Evans 1878-1945
The Welsh Miner

*H*elen of the roads,
The mountain ways of Wales
And the Mabinogion tales
Is one of the true gods.

Edward Thomas 1878-1917

Roads

*O*ne road leads to London,
  One road leads to Wales,
My road leads me seawards
  To the white dipping sails.

John Masefield 1878-1967

Roadways

*W*ales is a beautiful mother, but she can
be a dangerously possessive wife.

Rhys Davies 1901-78

My Wales

There is still a primitive shine on Wales;
one can smell the old world there still, and
it is not a dead aroma.

Rhys Davies 1901-78

My Wales

A vineyard placed in my care is Wales,
my country,
To deliver unto my children
And my children's children
Intact, an eternal heritage.

Saunders Lewis 1893-1985

Buchedd Garmon

O timbers from Norway and muscles
  from Wales,
Be ready for another shift and believe in
  co-operation,
Though pit-wheels are frowning at old
  misfortunes
And girders remember disasters of old;
O what is man that coal should be so
  careless of him,
And what is coal that so much blood
  should be upon it?

Idris Davies 1905-53

Gwalia Deserta

*W*e gave our masterpiece to history in
our country's MPs.

Saunders Lewis 1893-1985

Y Dilyw, 1935

He scorned his land, his tongue denied;
Nor Welsh nor English, lived and died
A bastard mule, and made his own
Each mulish fault save one alone:
Dic somehow got, that prince of fools,
A vast vile progeny of mules.

T J Thomas (Sarnicol) 1873-1945

Dic Si n Dafydd

Owain Glyndwr said all there is to be said
for this country hundreds of years ago.
Wales for the Welsh. More of him and less
of Mr Marx, please.

Richard Llewellyn 1906-83

How Green Was My Valley

How Green was my Valley, then, and the
Valley of them that have gone.

Richard Llewellyn 1906-83

How Green Was My Valley

*T*he Welsh are a nation of toughs, rogues, and poetic humbugs, vivid in their speech, impulsive in behaviour, and riddled with a sly and belligerent tribalism.

V S Pritchett 1900-97
in *The New Statesman*

*S*t Michael, who loves the hills,
  pray for Wales,
St. Michael, friend of the sick, remember us.

Saunders Lewis 1893-1985
Haf Bach Mihangel

*L*ightning is different in Wales.

Keidrych Rhys 1915-87
Youth

*T*he strength of the commom man was
always the strength of Wales.

Keidrych Rhys 1915-87
Tragic Guilt

I lost my native language
For the one the Saxon spake
By going to school by order
For education's sake.

Idris Davies 1905-53
I Was Born in Rhymney

I am a Welshman with an
international accent.

Arthur Horner 1894-1968
attributed

We'll keep a welcome in the hillsides,
We'll keep a welcome in the vales,
This land you knew will still be singing
When you come home again to Wales.

This land of song will keep a welcome
And with a love that never fails,
We'll kiss away each hour of hiraeth
When you come home again to Wales.

Lyn Joshua and James Harper 1949
We'll keep a welcome in the hillsides

I feel the claws of Wales tearing
at my heart.

T H Parry-Williams 1887-1975
Hon

*W*e were a people bred on legends,
Warming our hands at the red past.

R S Thomas (born 1913)

Welsh History

*W*e were a people, and are so yet.
When we have finished quarrelling for
    crumbs
Under the table, or gnawing the bones
Of a dead culture, we will arise,
Armed, but not in the old way.

R S Thomas (born 1913)

Welsh History

*T*here is no present in Wales,

And no future;

There is only the past,

Brittle with relics,

Wind-bitten towers and castles

With sham ghosts;

Mouldering quarries and mines;

And an impotent people,

Sick with inbreeding,

Worrying the carcase of an old song.

R S Thomas (born 1913)

Welsh Landscape

*T*here's holy holy people
They are in capel bach --
They don't like surpliced choirs,
They don't like Sospan Fach . . .

And when they go to Heaven,
They won't like that too well,
For the music will be sweeter
Than the music played in Hell.

Idris Davies 1905-53

Capel Calvin

*P*ay a penny for my singing torch,
O my sisters, my brothers of the land of
    my mothers,
The land of our fathers, our troubles,
    our dreams,
The land of Llewellyn and Shoni
    bach Shinkin,
The land of the sermons that pebble
    the streams,
The land of the englyn and Crawshay's
    old engine,
The land that is sometimes as proud as
    she seems.

Idris Davies 1905-53

Land of my Mothers

*W*e close the door
On Wales and backwards, eastwards,
   from the source
Of such clear water, leave that altered
   shore
Of gulls and psalms, of green and gold
   largesse.

Louis MacNeice 1907-63
Autumn Sequel

*W*ithin the whispering gallery of St. Paul's
The merest whisper travels round the walls;
But in the parts where I was born and bred
Folk hear things long before they're even
   said.

A G Prys-Jones 1888-1987
Quite So

*W*e are not wholly bad or good
Who live our lives under Milk Wood,
And Thou, I know, wilt be the first
To see our best side, not our worst.

Dylan Thomas 1914-53

Under Milk Wood

*P*raise the Lord! We are a musical nation.

Dylan Thomas 1914-53

Under Milk Wood

*W*elsh is of this soil, this island, the senior
language of the men of Britain;
and Welsh is beautiful.

J R R Tolkien 1892-1973

The O'Donnell Lecture 1955

Wales, which I have never seen,
Is gloomy, mountainous and green.

Rolfe Humphries 1894-1969

For My Ancestors

They practise magic out of season,
They hate the English with good reason,
Nor do they trust the Irish more,
And find the Scots an utter bore.

Rolfe Humphries 1894-1969

For My Ancestors

*T*here are still parts of Wales where the only concession to gaiety is a striped shroud.

Gwyn Thomas 1913-81

in *Punch, 1958*

*W*hen an Englishman has a pint too many, he wants to fight, or make love, or subside into the womb of smutty anecdote; but when the Welshman stands beside the bar he, apparently, wants to sing.

James Morris (born 1926)

Welshness in Wales

*E*ven God had a Welsh name:
We spoke to him in the old language;
He was to have a peculiar care
For the Welsh people.

R S Thomas (born 1913)

A Welsh Testament

*C*old water, Dewi,
Is not for our palate,
We keep your festival
With foolish mirth,
Self-praise and self-pity,
Dragons and flagons,
But none who will suffer
For Wales in her dearth.

Harri Webb 1920-65

Ty Ddewi

Always I feel the cold and cutting blast
Of winds that blow about my native hills,
And know that I can never be content
In this or any other continent
Until with my frosty fathers I am at last
Back in the old country that kills and sings.

T H Jones 1921-65

Land of my Fathers

Two lands at last connected
Across the waters wide,
And all the tolls collected
On the English side.

Harri Webb 1920-94

Ode to the Severn Bridge

*N*ever forget your Welsh.

Anonymous c.1970
advertisement for beer

*W*ales! Whales? D'you mean da fish, or dem singing bastards?

Anonymous
New York taxi-driver c. 1976

*W*hat Wales needs, and has always lacked most Is, instead of an eastern boundary, an East Coast.

Harri Webb 1920-94
Our Scientists are Working on It

*I*f Wales were to be rolled out as flat as England, it would be the bigger country of the two.

Anonymous c.1978

*W*e are still here! We are still here! Despite everyone and everything, We are still here!

Dafydd Iwan 1943-
Yma o Hyd

*H*appiness is knowing you are Welsh.

Anonymous
car-sticker c.1980